Blastoff! Readers are carefully developed by literacy experts to build reading stamina and move students toward fluency by combining standards-based content with developmentally appropriate text.

LEVELS

 Level 1 provides the most support through repetition of high-frequency words, light text, predictable sentence patterns, and strong visual support.

 Level 2 offers early readers a bit more challenge through varied sentences, increased text load, and text-supportive special features.

 Level 3 advances early-fluent readers toward fluency through increased text load, less reliance on photos, advancing concepts, longer sentences, and more complex special features.

★ **Blastoff! Universe**

Reading Level

 Grade K

 Grades 1–3

 Grade 4

This edition first published in 2025 by Bellwether Media, Inc.

No part of this publication may be reproduced in whole or in part without written permission of the publisher. For information regarding permission, write to Bellwether Media, Inc., Attention: Permissions Department, 6012 Blue Circle Drive, Minnetonka, MN 55343.

Library of Congress Cataloging-in-Publication Data

LC record for Jealous available at: https://lccn.loc.gov/2024014725

Text copyright © 2025 by Bellwether Media, Inc. BLASTOFF! READERS and associated logos are trademarks and/or registered trademarks of Bellwether Media, Inc. Bellwether Media is a division of Chrysalis Education Group.

Editor: Rebecca Sabelko   Designer: Andrea Schneider

Printed in the United States of America, North Mankato, MN.

Table of Contents

At a Birthday Party   4
What Is Jealousy?   6
Being Jealous   14
Glossary   22
To Learn More   23
Index   24

At a Birthday Party

Ellie is at Luke's birthday party.
Luke opens presents.
Ellie feels jealous.

What Is Jealousy?

Jealousy is an emotion. You might feel scared of losing something. You may be **envious**.

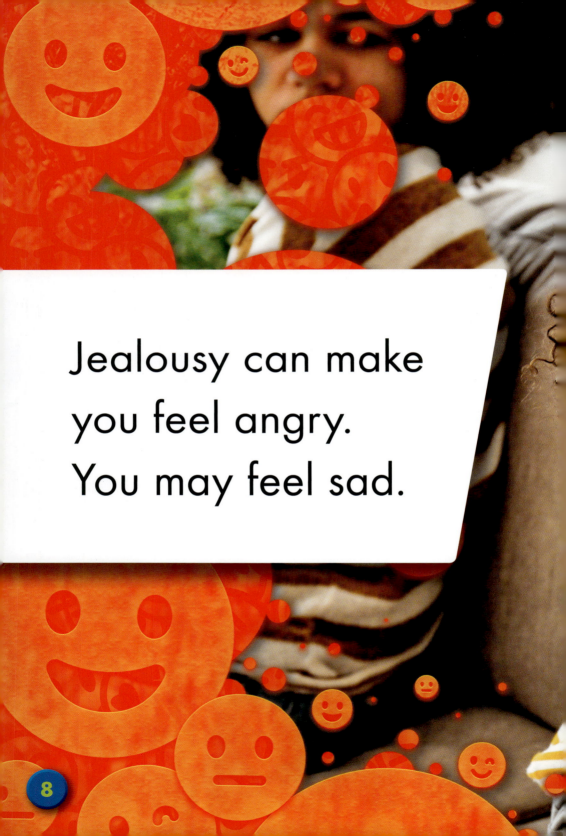

Jealousy can make you feel angry. You may feel sad.

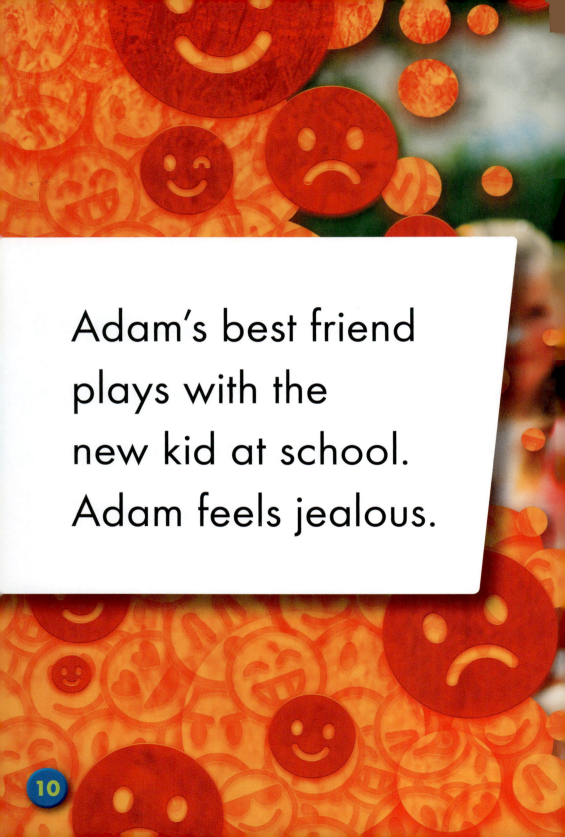

Adam's best friend plays with the new kid at school. Adam feels jealous.

Eloise's team lost. She feels envious of the winning team.

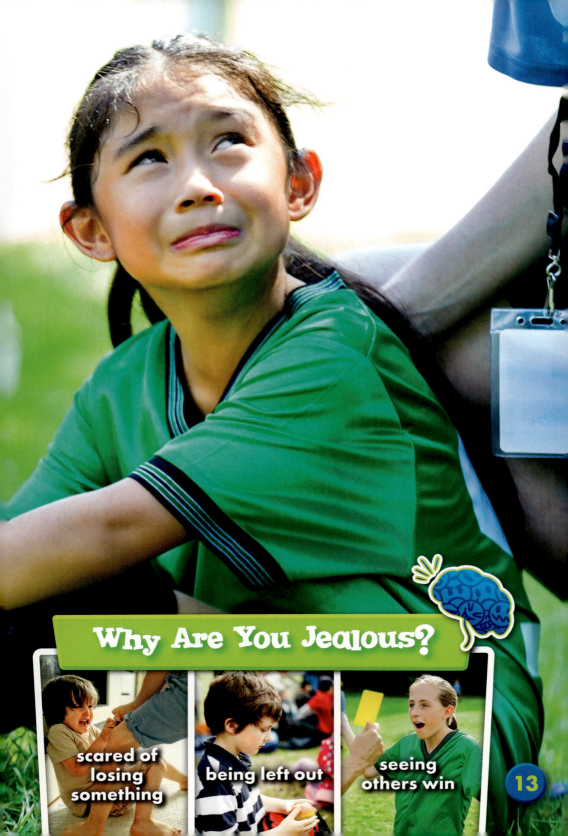

Why Are You Jealous?

scared of losing something

being left out

seeing others win

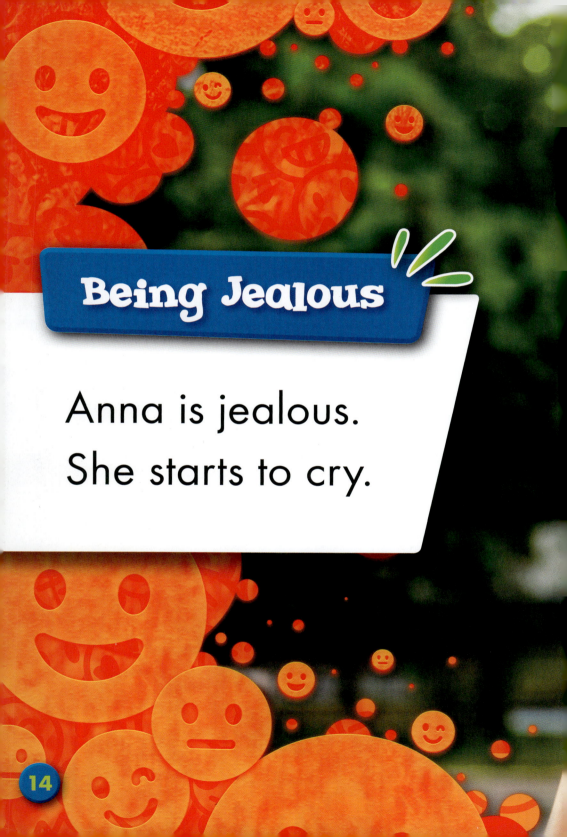

Being Jealous

Anna is jealous.
She starts to cry.

Levi is envious. He **frowns** and crosses his arms.

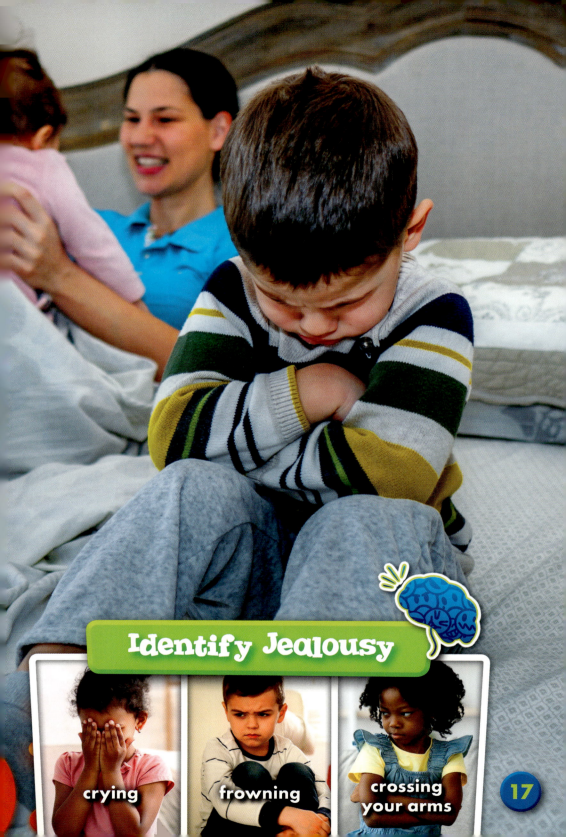

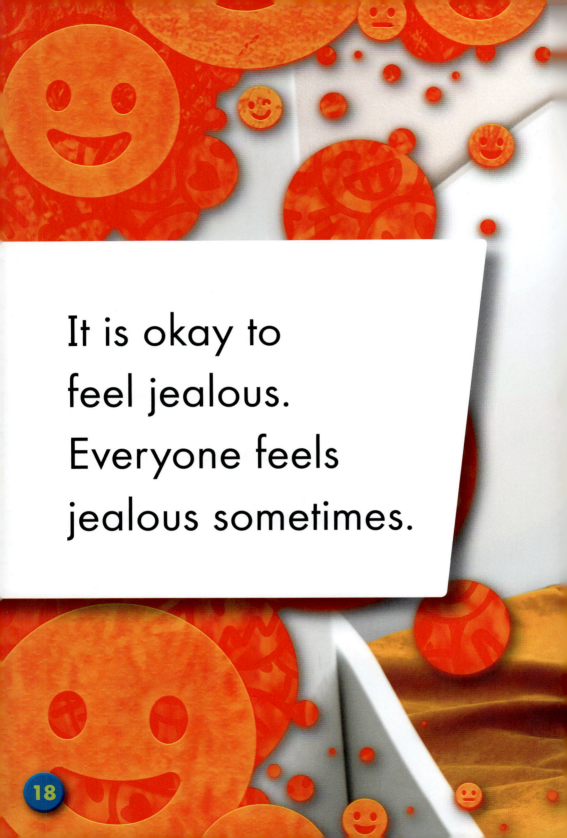

It is okay to feel jealous. Everyone feels jealous sometimes.

Talk to an adult you trust. Practice feeling **grateful**. Remember that you are **unique**!

Glossary

envious
wanting something that someone else has

grateful
thankful

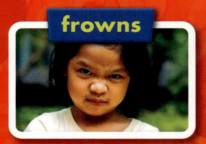

frowns
brings eyebrows together, showing a person is upset or thinking

unique
one of a kind

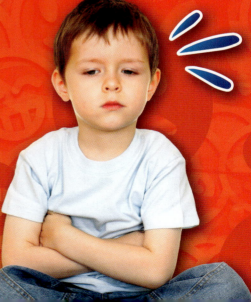

To Learn More

AT THE LIBRARY

Chang, Kirsten. *Understanding Emotions*. Minneapolis, Minn.: Bellwether Media, 2022.

Finne, Stephanie. *I Feel Jealous*. Minneapolis, Minn.: Jump!, 2022.

Wood, John. *The Green Book: What to Do When You're Jealous*. Minneapolis, Minn.: Bearport Publishing Company, 2023.

ON THE WEB

FACTSURFER

Factsurfer.com gives you a safe, fun way to find more information.

1. Go to www.factsurfer.com.

2. Enter "jealous" into the search box and click 🔍.

3. Select your book cover to see a list of related content.

Index

adult, 20
angry, 8
arms, 16
cry, 14
emotion, 6
envious, 6, 12, 16
feels, 4, 6, 8, 10, 12, 18, 20
friend, 10
frowns, 16
grateful, 20
identify jealousy, 17
party, 4
plays, 10

presents, 4
question, 21
sad, 8
scared, 6
school, 10
team, 12
unique, 20
why are you jealous, 13

The images in this book are reproduced through the courtesy of: kwanchai.c, front cover (jealous child); M_Agency, front cover (background); kwanchaichaiudom, p. 3; shironosov, pp. 4-5; mariakray, pp. 6-7; evrymmnt, pp. 8-9; BearFotos, pp. 10-11; SDI Productions, pp. 12-13, 13 (seeing others win); Anastasia Amraeva, p. 13 (scared of losing something); Eric Cote, p. 13 (being left out); Sinenkiy, pp. 14-15; freemixer, pp. 16-17; Prostock-studio, p. 17 (crying, crossing your arms); New Africa, p. 17 (frowning); Mariakray, pp. 18-19; CihatDeniz, pp. 20-21; MiniStocker, p. 22 (envious); Prot Tachapanit, p. 22 (frowns); Monkey Business Images, p. 22 (grateful); wavebreakmedia, p. 22 (unique); Monika Adamczyk, p. 22 (jealous child).